Angel On My Shoulder

JOURNAL

Your Angel will guide you through your journey of journaling

As You Begin Your Journey Begin with Prayer

To Kim   the Beginning
Prayer is the Beginning
Brenda

Angel On My Shoulder

Journal

A
  O
    M
      S

A
O M
  S

Brenda Gallow
2010

Take Control

Get ready for the first day of your new beginning

DATE:
TIME:

Step forward with your best foot first

Your goal is to maximize your life

GOD
YOU
FAMILY
WORK

God protects you

Trickle down effect

After each entry take time to reflect and analyze your day so the next will be better

What did you do to have a better _____

Please try not to leave a page blank in your journal

At any given moment the SPIRIT will move you Write down what's on your mind this is

your **JOURNAL**  Whether it's negative or positive **IT'S YOUR THOUGHTS**

Keeping a journal most likely will help you follow through with your life long goals

Out of your journal may come a **BOOK**
                    PICTURE
               MUSIC
                MOVIE
               FAMILY
               SCHOOL...
                            the dream you never accomplished

Getting Started
Date:
Maximize your life

This is the beginning of a new beginning of your life
Your best life
Your Best Health
Your Best Finance
Your Best way with GOD

Begin with Thank You he woke me up
Remember There is no time for negativity
In order to go forward Let go of the worries
No it's not going to be easy but, one day at a time
This is why you have this journal; **AN ANGEL IS ON YOUR SHOULDER**

Having a bad day *NO* you're having a bad *MOMENT*

Stop, breathe, take a **DEEP** breath and smile, smell the roses and say

THE DEVIL IS A LIAR this is my best day

Don't forget to journal all your thoughts

<u>Sample:</u>

Date: <u>10/15/2010</u>

This is how my day went... <u>well</u>

My sleep... <u>was good</u>

My stress level... <u>was high</u>

My mood... <u>okay</u>

My environment... <u>moody</u>

Breakfast... <u>didn't eat</u>

Snack... <u>snickers</u>

Lunch... <u>rice chicken veggies</u>

Dinner... <u>didn't eat</u>

Snack... <u>yogurt</u>

Water Consumption... _____1/2 gallon_____

This is how I plan to have a better day ... <u>keep negativity away smile</u>

My goal for the day...<u>give encouraging words</u>

Challenges anticipated... <u>bills work</u>

My best choice of the day... <u>saying I love you to my son calling my family</u>

Date: _____

This is how my day went… _____

My sleep… _____

My stress level… _____

My mood… _____

My environment… _____

Breakfast… _____

Snack… _____

Lunch… _____

Dinner… _____

Snack… _____

Water Consumption… _____

This is how I plan to have a better day … _____

My goal for the day… _____

Challenges anticipated… _____

My best choice of the day… _____

Date: _____

This is how my day went... _____

My sleep... _____

My stress level... _____

My mood... _____

My environment... _____

Breakfast... _____

Snack... _____

Lunch... _____

Dinner... _____

Snack... _____

Water Consumption... _____

This is how I plan to have a better day ... _____

My goal for the day... _____

Challenges anticipated... _____

My best choice of the day... _____

Date: _____

This is how my day went... _____

My sleep... _____

My stress level... _____

My mood... _____

My environment... _____

Breakfast... _____

Snack... _____

Lunch... _____

Dinner... _____

Snack... _____

Water Consumption... _____

This is how I plan to have a better day ... _____

My goal for the day... _____

Challenges anticipated... _____

My best choice of the day... _____

Date: _____

This is how my day went... _____

My sleep... _____

My stress level... _____

My mood... _____

My environment... _____

Breakfast... _____

Snack... _____

Lunch... _____

Dinner... _____

Snack... _____

Water Consumption... _____

This is how I plan to have a better day ... _____

My goal for the day... _____

Challenges anticipated... _____

My best choice of the day... _____

Date: _____

This is how my day went... _____

My sleep... _____

My stress level... _____

My mood... _____

My environment... _____

Breakfast... _____

Snack... _____

Lunch... _____

Dinner... _____

Snack... _____

Water Consumption... _____

This is how I plan to have a better day ... _____

My goal for the day... _____

Challenges anticipated... _____

My best choice of the day... _____

Date: _____

This is how my day went… _____

My sleep… _____

My stress level… _____

My mood… _____

My environment… _____

Breakfast… _____

Snack… _____

Lunch… _____

Dinner… _____

Snack… _____

Water Consumption… _____

This is how I plan to have a better day … _____

My goal for the day… _____

Challenges anticipated… _____

My best choice of the day… _____

Date: _____

This is how my day went… _____

My sleep… _____

My stress level… _____

My mood… _____

My environment… _____

Breakfast… _____

Snack… _____

Lunch… _____

Dinner… _____

Snack… _____

Water Consumption… _____

This is how I plan to have a better day … _____

My goal for the day… _____

Challenges anticipated… _____

My best choice of the day… _____

SAMPLE

This week… was <u>better than I thought it would be</u>

Sleep… <u>my sleep is getting better</u>

Stress level… <u>still high working on it</u>

Mood… <u>up and down</u>

Environment… <u>better</u>

Breakfast… <u>eating breakfast now</u>

Lunch… <u>my biggest meal</u>

Dinner… <u>making it a light meal</u>

Snack… <u>fruit</u>

Water consumption… <u>trying to get to a gallon a day</u>

The week was <u>good 5</u>

I need to improve on… <u>my stress level eating better exercising</u>

You rate yourself. Good/Bad, scale 1-10, yes/no, happy/sad, long short.
Did you eat the right foods, did you drink water? How was your stress level?

This week my…

Sleep: _____

Stress level: _____

Mood: _____

Environment: _____

Breakfast: _____

Lunch: _____

Dinner: _____

Snack: _____

Water consumption: _____

The week was _____

I need to improve on…

You rate yourself. Good/Bad, scale 1-10, yes/no, happy/sad, long short.
Did you eat the right foods, did you drink water? How was your stress level?

Date: _____

This is how my day went... _____

My sleep... _____

My stress level... _____

My mood... _____

My environment... _____

Breakfast... _____

Snack... _____

Lunch... _____

Dinner... _____

Snack... _____

Water Consumption... _____

This is how I plan to have a better day ... _____

My goal for the day... _____

Challenges anticipated... _____

My best choice of the day... _____

Date: _____

This is how my day went... _____

My sleep... _____

My stress level... _____

My mood... _____

My environment... _____

Breakfast... _____

Snack... _____

Lunch... _____

Dinner... _____

Snack... _____

Water Consumption... _____

This is how I plan to have a better day ... _____

My goal for the day... _____

Challenges anticipated... _____

My best choice of the day... _____

Date: _____

This is how my day went... _____

My sleep... _____

My stress level... _____

My mood... _____

My environment... _____

Breakfast... _____

Snack... _____

Lunch... _____

Dinner... _____

Snack... _____

Water Consumption... _____

This is how I plan to have a better day ... _____

My goal for the day... _____

Challenges anticipated... _____

My best choice of the day... _____

Date: _____

This is how my day went... _____

My sleep... _____

My stress level... _____

My mood... _____

My environment... _____

Breakfast... _____

Snack... _____

Lunch... _____

Dinner... _____

Snack... _____

Water Consumption... _____

This is how I plan to have a better day ... _____

My goal for the day... _____

Challenges anticipated... _____

My best choice of the day... _____

Date: _____

This is how my day went... _____

My sleep... _____

My stress level... _____

My mood... _____

My environment... _____

Breakfast... _____

Snack... _____

Lunch... _____

Dinner... _____

Snack... _____

Water Consumption... _____

This is how I plan to have a better day ... _____

My goal for the day... _____

Challenges anticipated... _____

My best choice of the day... _____

Date: _____

This is how my day went... _____

My sleep... _____

My stress level... _____

My mood... _____

My environment... _____

Breakfast... _____

Snack... _____

Lunch... _____

Dinner... _____

Snack... _____

Water Consumption... _____

This is how I plan to have a better day ... _____

My goal for the day... _____

Challenges anticipated... _____

My best choice of the day... _____

Date: _____

This is how my day went... _____

My sleep... _____

My stress level... _____

My mood... _____

My environment... _____

Breakfast... _____

Snack... _____

Lunch... _____

Dinner... _____

Snack... _____

Water Consumption... _____

This is how I plan to have a better day ... _____

My goal for the day... _____

Challenges anticipated... _____

My best choice of the day... _____

This week my…

Sleep: _____

Stress level: _____

Mood: _____

Environment: _____

Breakfast: _____

Lunch: _____

Dinner: _____

Snack: _____

Water consumption: _____

The week was _____

I need to improve on…

You rate yourself. Good/Bad, scale 1-10, yes/no, happy/sad, long short.
Did you eat the right foods, did you drink water? How was your stress level?

Date: _____

This is how my day went... _____

My sleep... _____

My stress level... _____

My mood... _____

My environment... _____

Breakfast... _____

Snack... _____

Lunch... _____

Dinner... _____

Snack... _____

Water Consumption... _____

This is how I plan to have a better day ... _____

My goal for the day... _____

Challenges anticipated... _____

My best choice of the day... _____

Date: _____

This is how my day went... _____

My sleep... _____

My stress level... _____

My mood... _____

My environment... _____

Breakfast... _____

Snack... _____

Lunch... _____

Dinner... _____

Snack... _____

Water Consumption... _____

This is how I plan to have a better day ... _____

My goal for the day... _____

Challenges anticipated... _____

My best choice of the day... _____

Date: _____

This is how my day went... _____

My sleep... _____

My stress level... _____

My mood... _____

My environment... _____

Breakfast... _____

Snack... _____

Lunch... _____

Dinner... _____

Snack... _____

Water Consumption... _____

This is how I plan to have a better day ... _____

My goal for the day... _____

Challenges anticipated... _____

My best choice of the day... _____

Date: _____

This is how my day went... _____

My sleep... _____

My stress level... _____

My mood... _____

My environment... _____

Breakfast... _____

Snack... _____

Lunch... _____

Dinner... _____

Snack... _____

Water Consumption... _____

This is how I plan to have a better day ... _____

My goal for the day... _____

Challenges anticipated... _____

My best choice of the day... _____

Date: _____

This is how my day went... _____

My sleep... _____

My stress level... _____

My mood... _____

My environment... _____

Breakfast... _____

Snack... _____

Lunch... _____

Dinner... _____

Snack... _____

Water Consumption... _____

This is how I plan to have a better day ... _____

My goal for the day... _____

Challenges anticipated... _____

My best choice of the day... _____

Date: _____

This is how my day went... _____

My sleep... _____

My stress level... _____

My mood... _____

My environment... _____

Breakfast... _____

Snack... _____

Lunch... _____

Dinner... _____

Snack... _____

Water Consumption... _____

This is how I plan to have a better day ... _____

My goal for the day... _____

Challenges anticipated... _____

My best choice of the day... _____

Date: _____

This is how my day went... _____

My sleep... _____

My stress level... _____

My mood... _____

My environment... _____

Breakfast... _____

Snack... _____

Lunch... _____

Dinner... _____

Snack... _____

Water Consumption... _____

This is how I plan to have a better day ... _____

My goal for the day... _____

Challenges anticipated... _____

My best choice of the day... _____

This week my…

       Sleep: _____

       Stress level: _____

       Mood: _____

       Environment: _____

       Breakfast: _____

       Lunch: _____

       Dinner: _____

       Snack: _____

       Water consumption: _____

              The week was _____

I need to improve on…_____

You rate yourself. Good/Bad, scale 1-10, yes/no, happy/sad, long short.
Did you eat the right foods, did you drink water? How was your stress level?

Date: _____

This is how my day went… _____

My sleep… _____

My stress level… _____

My mood… _____

My environment… _____

Breakfast… _____

Snack… _____

Lunch… _____

Dinner… _____

Snack… _____

Water Consumption… _____

This is how I plan to have a better day … _____

My goal for the day… _____

Challenges anticipated… _____

My best choice of the day… _____

Date: _____

This is how my day went... _____

My sleep... _____

My stress level... _____

My mood... _____

My environment... _____

Breakfast... _____

Snack... _____

Lunch... _____

Dinner... _____

Snack... _____

Water Consumption... _____

This is how I plan to have a better day ... _____

My goal for the day... _____

Challenges anticipated... _____

My best choice of the day... _____

Date: _____

This is how my day went… _____

My sleep… _____

My stress level… _____

My mood… _____

My environment… _____

Breakfast… _____

Snack… _____

Lunch… _____

Dinner… _____

Snack… _____

Water Consumption… _____

This is how I plan to have a better day … _____

My goal for the day… _____

Challenges anticipated… _____

My best choice of the day… _____

Date: _____

This is how my day went... _____

My sleep... _____

My stress level... _____

My mood... _____

My environment... _____

Breakfast... _____

Snack... _____

Lunch... _____

Dinner... _____

Snack... _____

Water Consumption... _____

This is how I plan to have a better day ... _____

My goal for the day... _____

Challenges anticipated... _____

My best choice of the day... _____

Date: _____

This is how my day went... _____

My sleep... _____

My stress level... _____

My mood... _____

My environment... _____

Breakfast... _____

Snack... _____

Lunch... _____

Dinner... _____

Snack... _____

Water Consumption... _____

This is how I plan to have a better day ... _____

My goal for the day... _____

Challenges anticipated... _____

My best choice of the day... _____

Date: _____

This is how my day went... _____

My sleep... _____

My stress level... _____

My mood... _____

My environment... _____

Breakfast... _____

Snack... _____

Lunch... _____

Dinner... _____

Snack... _____

Water Consumption... _____

This is how I plan to have a better day ... _____

My goal for the day... _____

Challenges anticipated... _____

My best choice of the day... _____

Date: _____

This is how my day went... _____

My sleep... _____

My stress level... _____

My mood... _____

My environment... _____

Breakfast... _____

Snack... _____

Lunch... _____

Dinner... _____

Snack... _____

Water Consumption... _____

This is how I plan to have a better day ... _____

My goal for the day... _____

Challenges anticipated... _____

My best choice of the day... _____

This week my…

Sleep: _____

Stress level: _____

Mood: _____

Environment: _____

Breakfast: _____

Lunch: _____

Dinner: _____

Snack: _____

Water consumption: _____

The week was _____

I need to improve on… _____

You rate yourself. Good/Bad, scale 1-10, yes/no, happy/sad, long short.
Did you eat the right foods, did you drink water? How was your stress level?

Plan meals for the week
        Designate a day for yourself
        Get a planner organize your tasks
Do something different every day

While your brushing your teeth
        Walk in place, jog do squats
                This is part of your exercise
At work sitting at your desk
        Neck rolls
                Shoulder shrug
                        Ankle swirls

During Lunch
        Stretch
                If you can walk 10 minutes it's great if you can do more GO FOR IT
At home
        I know your saying I'm tired
                But if you get everyone involved it won't be a task
                        It will be family fun time
        Have everyone write what exercise they enjoy
                And each day or that week that's the exercise that will be done

GOOD SOURCES OR PROTEIN, IRON, AND CALCIUM

Protein:
   Almonds, black beans, brown rice, cashews, garbanzo beans (chickpeas), kidney beans, lentils, lima beans, peanut butter, pinto beans, soybeans, tofu bran flakes, cashews,

Iron:
   Black beans, garbanzo beans (chickpeas), kidney beans, lentils, navy beans, oatmeal, raisins, spinach, tofu, whole wheat bread

Calcium:
   Almonds, black beans, broccoli, calcium-fortified orange juice, collard greens, kidney beans, mustard greens, pinto beans, tofu

STRAWBERRY SMOOTHIE
   Makes 2 cups
   1 cup frozen strawberries
   1 cup frozen banana chunks
   ½ cup to 1 cup soy or rice milk
Place all ingredients in a blender and process on high speed until smooth, 2 to 3 minutes, occasionally stopping the blender to move any unblended fruit to the center with a spatula.

Date: _____

This is how my day went... _____

My sleep... _____

My stress level... _____

My mood... _____

My environment... _____

Breakfast... _____

Snack... _____

Lunch... _____

Dinner... _____

Snack... _____

Water Consumption... _____

This is how I plan to have a better day ... _____

My goal for the day... _____

Challenges anticipated... _____

My best choice of the day... _____

Date: _____

This is how my day went... _____

My sleep... _____

My stress level... _____

My mood... _____

My environment... _____

Breakfast... _____

Snack... _____

Lunch... _____

Dinner... _____

Snack... _____

Water Consumption... _____

This is how I plan to have a better day ... _____

My goal for the day... _____

Challenges anticipated... _____

My best choice of the day... _____

Date: _____

This is how my day went... _____

My sleep... _____

My stress level... _____

My mood... _____

My environment... _____

Breakfast... _____

Snack... _____

Lunch... _____

Dinner... _____

Snack... _____

Water Consumption... _____

This is how I plan to have a better day ... _____

My goal for the day... _____

Challenges anticipated... _____

My best choice of the day... _____

Date: _____

This is how my day went... _____

My sleep... _____

My stress level... _____

My mood... _____

My environment... _____

Breakfast... _____

Snack... _____

Lunch... _____

Dinner... _____

Snack... _____

Water Consumption... _____

This is how I plan to have a better day ... _____

My goal for the day... _____

Challenges anticipated... _____

My best choice of the day... _____

Date: _____

This is how my day went... _____

My sleep... _____

My stress level... _____

My mood... _____

My environment... _____

Breakfast... _____

Snack... _____

Lunch... _____

Dinner... _____

Snack... _____

Water Consumption... _____

This is how I plan to have a better day ... _____

My goal for the day... _____

Challenges anticipated... _____

My best choice of the day... _____

Date: _____

This is how my day went… _____

My sleep… _____

My stress level… _____

My mood… _____

My environment… _____

Breakfast… _____

Snack… _____

Lunch… _____

Dinner… _____

Snack… _____

Water Consumption… _____

This is how I plan to have a better day … _____

My goal for the day… _____

Challenges anticipated… _____

My best choice of the day… _____

Date: _____

This is how my day went... _____

My sleep... _____

My stress level... _____

My mood... _____

My environment... _____

Breakfast... _____

Snack... _____

Lunch... _____

Dinner... _____

Snack... _____

Water Consumption... _____

This is how I plan to have a better day ... _____

My goal for the day... _____

Challenges anticipated... _____

My best choice of the day... _____

This week my…

     Sleep: _____

     Stress level: _____

     Mood: _____

     Environment: _____

     Breakfast: _____

     Lunch: _____

     Dinner: _____

     Snack: _____

     Water consumption: _____

               The week was _____

I need to improve on…

You rate yourself. Good/Bad, scale 1-10, yes/no, happy/sad, long short.
Did you eat the right foods, did you drink water? How was your stress level?
Now your on the right track to a better you

STILL CAN'T FIND TIME

What if the Doctor told you needed to take 30 minutes every morning and evening to relax, or you would have to be in the hospital for 1 month Would you do it

FOOD FOR THOUGHT
We as humans do what we want when we want and how we want to do it

You find time and money for what you feel is best at that moment

The President of the United States
Finds
Time to exercise and he has
A
Very busy schedule

Broccoli Salad

Total servings: 6
Serving size: 1 cup

Salad

 2 quarts water
 6 cups broccoli florets (about 2-3pounds)

Dressing

 1 Tablespoon corn oil
 2 Tablespoon sesame oil
 3 Tablespoon lite soy sauce
 ½ cup minced scallions
 3 garlic cloves, minced

1. In a large pot, bring the water to a boil. Add the broccoli and blanch for 2-3 minutes. Immediately drain the broccoli and then plunge it in a bowl of ice water to stop the cooking process. Drain again. Place in a large salad bowl.
2. Combine the dressing ingredients. Add it to the blanched broccoli and toss well. Refrigerate until ready to serve

REMEMBER NO JOURNAL PAGE SHOULD BE BLANK

Most people don't drink enough water, and do not remember the last time they did so.

What they can remember is the last time they had
a soda
coffee
Gatorade
Alcohol

BUT NOT WATER!!!

DRINK AT LEAST (8) EIGHT 8 OUNCE GLASSSES OF WATER PER DAY

<u>BE PROACTIVE</u>

EXERCISE START WITH WALKING BEGIN IN MODERATION

<u>BE PATIENT</u>

EVERYTHING TAKES TIME

BY NOT DRINKING ENOUGH WATER YOU WILL
BE CRANKY
SLUGGISH
SLEEPY
HAVE CLOUDY URINE
TIRED

DRINK YOUR WATER
Keep a bottle of water in your car
At your desk
Next to your bed
Sip whenever you can to reach your goal of 64 ounces a day
8 glasses of 8 ounces of water

Get stimulated

Dive into Fitness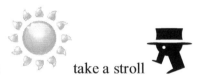

Strengthen your heart get toned and healthy
It's time to take a plunge into the nearest swimming pool
Swimming is less stress on the joints

Get some sun   take a stroll

HAVE A GOOD LAUGH

Date: _____

This is how my day went… _____

My sleep… _____

My stress level… _____

My mood… _____

My environment… _____

Breakfast… _____

Snack… _____

Lunch… _____

Dinner… _____

Snack… _____

Water Consumption… _____

This is how I plan to have a better day … _____

My goal for the day… _____

Challenges anticipated… _____

My best choice of the day… _____

Date: _____

This is how my day went... _____

My sleep... _____

My stress level... _____

My mood... _____

My environment... _____

Breakfast... _____

Snack... _____

Lunch... _____

Dinner... _____

Snack... _____

Water Consumption... _____

This is how I plan to have a better day ... _____

My goal for the day... _____

Challenges anticipated... _____

My best choice of the day... _____

Date: _____

This is how my day went… _____

My sleep… _____

My stress level… _____

My mood… _____

My environment… _____

Breakfast… _____

Snack… _____

Lunch… _____

Dinner… _____

Snack… _____

Water Consumption… _____

This is how I plan to have a better day … _____

My goal for the day… _____

Challenges anticipated… _____

My best choice of the day… _____

Date: _____

This is how my day went... _____

My sleep... _____

My stress level... _____

My mood... _____

My environment... _____

Breakfast... _____

Snack... _____

Lunch... _____

Dinner... _____

Snack... _____

Water Consumption... _____

This is how I plan to have a better day ... _____

My goal for the day... _____

Challenges anticipated... _____

My best choice of the day... _____

Date: _____

This is how my day went... _____

My sleep... _____

My stress level... _____

My mood... _____

My environment... _____

Breakfast... _____

Snack... _____

Lunch... _____

Dinner... _____

Snack... _____

Water Consumption... _____

This is how I plan to have a better day ... _____

My goal for the day... _____

Challenges anticipated... _____

My best choice of the day... _____

Date: _____

This is how my day went... _____

My sleep... _____

My stress level... _____

My mood... _____

My environment... _____

Breakfast... _____

Snack... _____

Lunch... _____

Dinner... _____

Snack... _____

Water Consumption... _____

This is how I plan to have a better day ... _____

My goal for the day... _____

Challenges anticipated... _____

My best choice of the day... _____

Date: _____

This is how my day went... _____

My sleep... _____

My stress level... _____

My mood... _____

My environment... _____

Breakfast... _____

Snack... _____

Lunch... _____

Dinner... _____

Snack... _____

Water Consumption... _____

This is how I plan to have a better day ... _____

My goal for the day... _____

Challenges anticipated... _____

My best choice of the day... _____

This week my…

     Sleep: _____

     Stress level: _____

     Mood: _____

     Environment: _____

     Breakfast: _____

     Lunch: _____

     Dinner: _____

     Snack: _____

     Water consumption: _____

             The week was _____

I need to improve on…

You rate yourself. Good/Bad, scale 1-10, yes/no, happy/sad, long short.
Did you eat the right foods, did you drink water? How was your stress level?

Snacks
- ➤ **Fresh fruit**
- ➤ **Mixed nuts**
- ➤ **Energy bar**
- ➤ **Baked pita wedges with hummus**
- ➤ **Yogurt**

Date: _____

This is how my day went... _____

My sleep... _____

My stress level... _____

My mood... _____

My environment... _____

Breakfast... _____

Snack... _____

Lunch... _____

Dinner... _____

Snack... _____

Water Consumption... _____

This is how I plan to have a better day ... _____

My goal for the day... _____

Challenges anticipated... _____

My best choice of the day... _____

Date: _____

This is how my day went… _____

My sleep… _____

My stress level… _____

My mood… _____

My environment… _____

Breakfast… _____

Snack… _____

Lunch… _____

Dinner… _____

Snack… _____

Water Consumption… _____

This is how I plan to have a better day … _____

My goal for the day… _____

Challenges anticipated… _____

My best choice of the day… _____

Date: _____

This is how my day went... _____

My sleep... _____

My stress level... _____

My mood... _____

My environment... _____

Breakfast... _____

Snack... _____

Lunch... _____

Dinner... _____

Snack... _____

Water Consumption... _____

This is how I plan to have a better day ... _____

My goal for the day... _____

Challenges anticipated... _____

My best choice of the day... _____

Date: _____

This is how my day went... _____

My sleep... _____

My stress level... _____

My mood... _____

My environment... _____

Breakfast... _____

Snack... _____

Lunch... _____

Dinner... _____

Snack... _____

Water Consumption... _____

This is how I plan to have a better day ... _____

My goal for the day... _____

Challenges anticipated... _____

My best choice of the day... _____

Date: _____

This is how my day went... _____

My sleep... _____

My stress level... _____

My mood... _____

My environment... _____

Breakfast... _____

Snack... _____

Lunch... _____

Dinner... _____

Snack... _____

Water Consumption... _____

This is how I plan to have a better day ... _____

My goal for the day... _____

Challenges anticipated... _____

My best choice of the day... _____

Date: _____

This is how my day went... _____

My sleep... _____

My stress level... _____

My mood... _____

My environment... _____

Breakfast... _____

Snack... _____

Lunch... _____

Dinner... _____

Snack... _____

Water Consumption... _____

This is how I plan to have a better day ... _____

My goal for the day... _____

Challenges anticipated... _____

My best choice of the day... _____

Date: _____

This is how my day went... _____

My sleep... _____

My stress level... _____

My mood... _____

My environment... _____

Breakfast... _____

Snack... _____

Lunch... _____

Dinner... _____

Snack... _____

Water Consumption... _____

This is how I plan to have a better day ... _____

My goal for the day... _____

Challenges anticipated... _____

My best choice of the day... _____

This week my…

Sleep: _____

Stress level: _____

Mood: _____

Environment: _____

Breakfast: _____

Lunch: _____

Dinner: _____

Snack: _____

Water consumption: _____

The week was _____

I need to improve on…

You rate yourself. Good/Bad, scale 1-10, yes/no, happy/sad, long short.
Did you eat the right foods, did you drink water? How was your stress level?

Do Not Disturb

SLEEP

REST

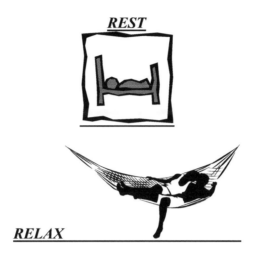

RELAX

The least effort of all is sleep
But it's the strongest activity

To have a healthy life reduce some stress
For any type of healing you have to rest

A good night's sleep does more than leave you feeling
Relax and refreshed in the morning
It's an important benefit

Date: _____

This is how my day went... _____

My sleep... _____

My stress level... _____

My mood... _____

My environment... _____

Breakfast... _____

Snack... _____

Lunch... _____

Dinner... _____

Snack... _____

Water Consumption... _____

This is how I plan to have a better day ... _____

My goal for the day... _____

Challenges anticipated... _____

My best choice of the day... _____

Date: _____

This is how my day went... _____

My sleep... _____

My stress level... _____

My mood... _____

My environment... _____

Breakfast... _____

Snack... _____

Lunch... _____

Dinner... _____

Snack... _____

Water Consumption... _____

This is how I plan to have a better day ... _____

My goal for the day... _____

Challenges anticipated... _____

My best choice of the day... _____

Date: _____

This is how my day went... _____

My sleep... _____

My stress level... _____

My mood... _____

My environment... _____

Breakfast... _____

Snack... _____

Lunch... _____

Dinner... _____

Snack... _____

Water Consumption... _____

This is how I plan to have a better day ... _____

My goal for the day... _____

Challenges anticipated... _____

My best choice of the day... _____

Date: _____

This is how my day went… _____

My sleep… _____

My stress level… _____

My mood… _____

My environment… _____

Breakfast… _____

Snack… _____

Lunch… _____

Dinner… _____

Snack… _____

Water Consumption… _____

This is how I plan to have a better day … _____

My goal for the day… _____

Challenges anticipated… _____

My best choice of the day… _____

Date: _____

This is how my day went... _____

My sleep... _____

My stress level... _____

My mood... _____

My environment... _____

Breakfast... _____

Snack... _____

Lunch... _____

Dinner... _____

Snack... _____

Water Consumption... _____

This is how I plan to have a better day ... _____

My goal for the day... _____

Challenges anticipated... _____

My best choice of the day... _____

Date: _____

This is how my day went... _____

My sleep... _____

My stress level... _____

My mood... _____

My environment... _____

Breakfast... _____

Snack... _____

Lunch... _____

Dinner... _____

Snack... _____

Water Consumption... _____

This is how I plan to have a better day ... _____

My goal for the day... _____

Challenges anticipated... _____

My best choice of the day... _____

This week my…

Sleep: _____

Stress level: _____

Mood: _____

Environment: _____

Breakfast: _____

Lunch: _____

Dinner: _____

Snack: _____

Water consumption: _____

The week was _____

I need to improve on…

You rate yourself. Good/Bad, scale 1-10, yes/no, happy/sad, long short.
Did you eat the right foods, did you drink water? How was your stress level?

BRAIN TEASERS
YOU WILL SEE ANOTHER
SET
LATER IN THE JOURNAL

SAY THE ALPHABET BACKWARDS
(Z,Y,X,W,V,U,T,S,R,Q,P,O,N,M,L,K,J,I,H,G,F,E,D,C,B,A)

TAKE A DIFFERENT ROUTE TO WORK/SCHOOL

LEARN A FORGIN LANGUAGE

LEARN A NEW WORD PER DAY, WEEK, OR MONTH

TAKE UP A HOBBY

LEARN TO DRIVE

LEARN TO SKI

LEARN TO DANCE

LEARN TO RIDE A BIKE

LEARN TO SWIM

LEARN TO CROCHET

LEARN TO KNIT

TAKE YOGA

Date: _____

This is how my day went... _____

My sleep... _____

My stress level... _____

My mood... _____

My environment... _____

Breakfast... _____

Snack... _____

Lunch... _____

Dinner... _____

Snack... _____

Water Consumption... _____

This is how I plan to have a better day ... _____

My goal for the day... _____

Challenges anticipated... _____

My best choice of the day... _____

Date: _____

This is how my day went... _____

My sleep... _____

My stress level... _____

My mood... _____

My environment... _____

Breakfast... _____

Snack... _____

Lunch... _____

Dinner... _____

Snack... _____

Water Consumption... _____

This is how I plan to have a better day ... _____

My goal for the day... _____

Challenges anticipated... _____

My best choice of the day... _____

Date: _____

This is how my day went... _____

My sleep... _____

My stress level... _____

My mood... _____

My environment... _____

Breakfast... _____

Snack... _____

Lunch... _____

Dinner... _____

Snack... _____

Water Consumption... _____

This is how I plan to have a better day ... _____

My goal for the day... _____

Challenges anticipated... _____

My best choice of the day... _____

Date: _____

This is how my day went... _____

My sleep... _____

My stress level... _____

My mood... _____

My environment... _____

Breakfast... _____

Snack... _____

Lunch... _____

Dinner... _____

Snack... _____

Water Consumption... _____

This is how I plan to have a better day ... _____

My goal for the day... _____

Challenges anticipated... _____

My best choice of the day... _____

Date: _____

This is how my day went... _____

My sleep... _____

My stress level... _____

My mood... _____

My environment... _____

Breakfast... _____

Snack... _____

Lunch... _____

Dinner... _____

Snack... _____

Water Consumption... _____

This is how I plan to have a better day ... _____

My goal for the day... _____

Challenges anticipated... _____

My best choice of the day... _____

Date: _____

This is how my day went... _____

My sleep... _____

My stress level... _____

My mood... _____

My environment... _____

Breakfast... _____

Snack... _____

Lunch... _____

Dinner... _____

Snack... _____

Water Consumption... _____

This is how I plan to have a better day ... _____

My goal for the day... _____

Challenges anticipated... _____

My best choice of the day... _____

Date: _____

This is how my day went… _____

My sleep… _____

My stress level… _____

My mood… _____

My environment… _____

Breakfast… _____

Snack… _____

Lunch… _____

Dinner… _____

Snack… _____

Water Consumption… _____

This is how I plan to have a better day … _____

My goal for the day… _____

Challenges anticipated… _____

My best choice of the day… _____

This week my…

     Sleep: _____

     Stress level: _____

     Mood: _____

     Environment: _____

     Breakfast: _____

     Lunch: _____

     Dinner: _____

     Snack: _____

     Water consumption: _____

              The week was _____

I need to improve on…

You rate yourself. Good/Bad, scale 1-10, yes/no, happy/sad, long short.
Did you eat the right foods, did you drink water? How was your stress level?

Stress

A little stress is a good thing When your body encounter a stressful situation your brain releases the stress hormone cortisol which shifts your body into fight or flight mode Your blood pressure rises your heart beats faster your pupils dilate and you can be ready to react When the stress passes your body returns to it's normal state

Relax

Mellow out with meditation
Give yourself a pep talk

LOOK IN THE MIRROR!!!

SMILE
SAY
YOU LOOK GOOD
YOU ARE DOING GREAT
HAVE POSITIVE THOUGHTS

Making change

How much is on your plate

Or is it a platter

Your challenge: I can't say no
Change: Smile and say I have a prior commitment

Be accountable

Watch your salt intake Nearly 80% of our salt intake comes from sodium in package foods So choosing healthy options can make a big difference
Reduce salt
Season popcorn with herbs instead of salt for more flavor
Rinse canned food such as beans to was away excess sodium

Reducing your sodium intake can be as easy as replacing a few of your packaged foods with fresh fruits and veggies A choice that can help fight inflammation and high blood pressure If you must add salt go with sea salt

Date: _____

This is how my day went… _____

My sleep… _____

My stress level… _____

My mood… _____

My environment… _____

Breakfast… _____

Snack… _____

Lunch… _____

Dinner… _____

Snack… _____

Water Consumption… _____

This is how I plan to have a better day … _____

My goal for the day… _____

Challenges anticipated… _____

My best choice of the day… _____

Date: _____

This is how my day went… _____

My sleep… _____

My stress level… _____

My mood… _____

My environment… _____

Breakfast… _____

Snack… _____

Lunch… _____

Dinner… _____

Snack… _____

Water Consumption… _____

This is how I plan to have a better day … _____

My goal for the day… _____

Challenges anticipated… _____

My best choice of the day… _____

Date: _____

This is how my day went... _____

My sleep... _____

My stress level... _____

My mood... _____

My environment... _____

Breakfast... _____

Snack... _____

Lunch... _____

Dinner... _____

Snack... _____

Water Consumption... _____

This is how I plan to have a better day ... _____

My goal for the day... _____

Challenges anticipated... _____

My best choice of the day... _____

Date: _____

This is how my day went... _____

My sleep... _____

My stress level... _____

My mood... _____

My environment... _____

Breakfast... _____

Snack... _____

Lunch... _____

Dinner... _____

Snack... _____

Water Consumption... _____

This is how I plan to have a better day ... _____

My goal for the day... _____

Challenges anticipated... _____

My best choice of the day... _____

Date: _____

This is how my day went... _____

My sleep... _____

My stress level... _____

My mood... _____

My environment... _____

Breakfast... _____

Snack... _____

Lunch... _____

Dinner... _____

Snack... _____

Water Consumption... _____

This is how I plan to have a better day ... _____

My goal for the day... _____

Challenges anticipated... _____

My best choice of the day... _____

Date: _____

This is how my day went... _____

My sleep... _____

My stress level... _____

My mood... _____

My environment... _____

Breakfast... _____

Snack... _____

Lunch... _____

Dinner... _____

Snack... _____

Water Consumption... _____

This is how I plan to have a better day ... _____

My goal for the day... _____

Challenges anticipated... _____

My best choice of the day... _____

Date: _____

This is how my day went... _____

My sleep... _____

My stress level... _____

My mood... _____

My environment... _____

Breakfast... _____

Snack... _____

Lunch... _____

Dinner... _____

Snack... _____

Water Consumption... _____

This is how I plan to have a better day ... _____

My goal for the day... _____

Challenges anticipated... _____

My best choice of the day... _____

This week my…

Sleep: _____

Stress level: _____

Mood: _____

Environment: _____

Breakfast: _____

Lunch: _____

Dinner: _____

Snack: _____

Water consumption: _____

The week was _____

I need to improve on…

You rate yourself. Good/Bad, scale 1-10, yes/no, happy/sad, long short.
 Did you eat the right foods, did you drink water? How was your stress level?

Date: _____

This is how my day went... _____

My sleep... _____

My stress level... _____

My mood... _____

My environment... _____

Breakfast... _____

Snack... _____

Lunch... _____

Dinner... _____

Snack... _____

Water Consumption... _____

This is how I plan to have a better day ... _____

My goal for the day... _____

Challenges anticipated... _____

My best choice of the day... _____

Date: _____

This is how my day went... _____

My sleep... _____

My stress level... _____

My mood... _____

My environment... _____

Breakfast... _____

Snack... _____

Lunch... _____

Dinner... _____

Snack... _____

Water Consumption... _____

This is how I plan to have a better day ... _____

My goal for the day... _____

Challenges anticipated... _____

My best choice of the day... _____

Date: _____

This is how my day went... _____

My sleep... _____

My stress level... _____

My mood... _____

My environment... _____

Breakfast... _____

Snack... _____

Lunch... _____

Dinner... _____

Snack... _____

Water Consumption... _____

This is how I plan to have a better day ... _____

My goal for the day... _____

Challenges anticipated... _____

My best choice of the day... _____

Date: _____

This is how my day went... _____

My sleep... _____

My stress level... _____

My mood... _____

My environment... _____

Breakfast... _____

Snack... _____

Lunch... _____

Dinner... _____

Snack... _____

Water Consumption... _____

This is how I plan to have a better day ... _____

My goal for the day... _____

Challenges anticipated... _____

My best choice of the day... _____

Date: _____

This is how my day went... _____

My sleep... _____

My stress level... _____

My mood... _____

My environment... _____

Breakfast... _____

Snack... _____

Lunch... _____

Dinner... _____

Snack... _____

Water Consumption... _____

This is how I plan to have a better day ... _____

My goal for the day... _____

Challenges anticipated... _____

My best choice of the day... _____

Date: _____

This is how my day went... _____

My sleep... _____

My stress level... _____

My mood... _____

My environment... _____

Breakfast... _____

Snack... _____

Lunch... _____

Dinner... _____

Snack... _____

Water Consumption... _____

This is how I plan to have a better day ... _____

My goal for the day... _____

Challenges anticipated... _____

My best choice of the day... _____

Date: _____

This is how my day went... _____

My sleep... _____

My stress level... _____

My mood... _____

My environment... _____

Breakfast... _____

Snack... _____

Lunch... _____

Dinner... _____

Snack... _____

Water Consumption... _____

This is how I plan to have a better day ... _____

My goal for the day... _____

Challenges anticipated... _____

My best choice of the day... _____

Date: _____

This is how my day went... _____

My sleep... _____

My stress level... _____

My mood... _____

My environment... _____

Breakfast... _____

Snack... _____

Lunch... _____

Dinner... _____

Snack... _____

Water Consumption... _____

This is how I plan to have a better day ... _____

My goal for the day... _____

Challenges anticipated... _____

My best choice of the day... _____

Date: _____

This is how my day went... _____

My sleep... _____

My stress level... _____

My mood... _____

My environment... _____

Breakfast... _____

Snack... _____

Lunch... _____

Dinner... _____

Snack... _____

Water Consumption... _____

This is how I plan to have a better day ... _____

My goal for the day... _____

Challenges anticipated... _____

My best choice of the day... _____

Date: _____

This is how my day went... _____

My sleep... _____

My stress level... _____

My mood... _____

My environment... _____

Breakfast... _____

Snack... _____

Lunch... _____

Dinner... _____

Snack... _____

Water Consumption... _____

This is how I plan to have a better day ... _____

My goal for the day... _____

Challenges anticipated... _____

My best choice of the day... _____

This week my…

Sleep: _____

Stress level: _____

Mood: _____

Environment: _____

Breakfast: _____

Lunch: _____

Dinner: _____

Snack: _____

Water consumption: _____

The week was _____

I need to improve on…

You rate yourself. Good/Bad, scale 1-10, yes/no, happy/sad, long short.
 Did you eat the right foods, did you drink water? How was your stress level?

Date: _____

This is how my day went... _____

My sleep... _____

My stress level... _____

My mood... _____

My environment... _____

Breakfast... _____

Snack... _____

Lunch... _____

Dinner... _____

Snack... _____

Water Consumption... _____

This is how I plan to have a better day ... _____

My goal for the day... _____

Challenges anticipated... _____

My best choice of the day... _____

Date: _____

This is how my day went... _____

My sleep... _____

My stress level... _____

My mood... _____

My environment... _____

Breakfast... _____

Snack... _____

Lunch... _____

Dinner... _____

Snack... _____

Water Consumption... _____

This is how I plan to have a better day ... _____

My goal for the day... _____

Challenges anticipated... _____

My best choice of the day... _____

Date: _____

This is how my day went... _____

My sleep... _____

My stress level... _____

My mood... _____

My environment... _____

Breakfast... _____

Snack... _____

Lunch... _____

Dinner... _____

Snack... _____

Water Consumption... _____

This is how I plan to have a better day ... _____

My goal for the day... _____

Challenges anticipated... _____

My best choice of the day... _____

Date: _____

This is how my day went… _____

My sleep… _____

My stress level… _____

My mood… _____

My environment… _____

Breakfast… _____

Snack… _____

Lunch… _____

Dinner… _____

Snack… _____

Water Consumption… _____

This is how I plan to have a better day … _____

My goal for the day… _____

Challenges anticipated… _____

My best choice of the day… _____

Date: _____

This is how my day went... _____

My sleep... _____

My stress level... _____

My mood... _____

My environment... _____

Breakfast... _____

Snack... _____

Lunch... _____

Dinner... _____

Snack... _____

Water Consumption... _____

This is how I plan to have a better day ... _____

My goal for the day... _____

Challenges anticipated... _____

My best choice of the day... _____

Date: _____

This is how my day went... _____

My sleep... _____

My stress level... _____

My mood... _____

My environment... _____

Breakfast... _____

Snack... _____

Lunch... _____

Dinner... _____

Snack... _____

Water Consumption... _____

This is how I plan to have a better day ... _____

My goal for the day... _____

Challenges anticipated... _____

My best choice of the day... _____

Date: _____

This is how my day went... _____

My sleep... _____

My stress level... _____

My mood... _____

My environment... _____

Breakfast... _____

Snack... _____

Lunch... _____

Dinner... _____

Snack... _____

Water Consumption... _____

This is how I plan to have a better day ... _____

My goal for the day... _____

Challenges anticipated... _____

My best choice of the day... _____

Date: _____

This is how my day went... _____

My sleep... _____

My stress level... _____

My mood... _____

My environment... _____

Breakfast... _____

Snack... _____

Lunch... _____

Dinner... _____

Snack... _____

Water Consumption... _____

This is how I plan to have a better day ... _____

My goal for the day... _____

Challenges anticipated... _____

My best choice of the day... _____

This week my…

Sleep: _____

Stress level: _____

Mood: _____

Environment: _____

Breakfast: _____

Lunch: _____

Dinner: _____

Snack: _____

Water consumption: _____

The week was _____

I need to improve on…

You rate yourself. Good/Bad, scale 1-10, yes/no, happy/sad, long short.
Did you eat the right foods, did you drink water? How was your stress level?

Focus on all of the positive things that happen
Give your brain a rest
Be happy
Healthy
Joyful
And most of all
Love you for God made you for a reason

Date: _____

This is how my day went... _____

My sleep... _____

My stress level... _____

My mood... _____

My environment... _____

Breakfast... _____

Snack... _____

Lunch... _____

Dinner... _____

Snack... _____

Water Consumption... _____

This is how I plan to have a better day ... _____

My goal for the day... _____

Challenges anticipated... _____

My best choice of the day... _____

Date: _____

This is how my day went... _____

My sleep... _____

My stress level... _____

My mood... _____

My environment... _____

Breakfast... _____

Snack... _____

Lunch... _____

Dinner... _____

Snack... _____

Water Consumption... _____

This is how I plan to have a better day ... _____

My goal for the day... _____

Challenges anticipated... _____

My best choice of the day... _____

Date: _____

This is how my day went... _____

My sleep... _____

My stress level... _____

My mood... _____

My environment... _____

Breakfast... _____

Snack... _____

Lunch... _____

Dinner... _____

Snack... _____

Water Consumption... _____

This is how I plan to have a better day ... _____

My goal for the day... _____

Challenges anticipated... _____

My best choice of the day... _____

Date: _____

This is how my day went… _____

My sleep… _____

My stress level… _____

My mood… _____

My environment… _____

Breakfast… _____

Snack… _____

Lunch… _____

Dinner… _____

Snack… _____

Water Consumption… _____

This is how I plan to have a better day … _____

My goal for the day… _____

Challenges anticipated… _____

My best choice of the day… _____

Date: _____

This is how my day went... _____

My sleep... _____

My stress level... _____

My mood... _____

My environment... _____

Breakfast... _____

Snack... _____

Lunch... _____

Dinner... _____

Snack... _____

Water Consumption... _____

This is how I plan to have a better day ... _____

My goal for the day... _____

Challenges anticipated... _____

My best choice of the day... _____

Date: _____

This is how my day went… _____

My sleep… _____

My stress level… _____

My mood… _____

My environment… _____

Breakfast… _____

Snack… _____

Lunch… _____

Dinner… _____

Snack… _____

Water Consumption… _____

This is how I plan to have a better day … _____

My goal for the day… _____

Challenges anticipated… _____

My best choice of the day… _____

Date: _____

This is how my day went... _____

My sleep... _____

My stress level... _____

My mood... _____

My environment... _____

Breakfast... _____

Snack... _____

Lunch... _____

Dinner... _____

Snack... _____

Water Consumption... _____

This is how I plan to have a better day ... _____

My goal for the day... _____

Challenges anticipated... _____

My best choice of the day... _____

Date: _____

This is how my day went… _____

My sleep… _____

My stress level… _____

My mood… _____

My environment… _____

Breakfast… _____

Snack… _____

Lunch… _____

Dinner… _____

Snack… _____

Water Consumption… _____

This is how I plan to have a better day … _____

My goal for the day… _____

Challenges anticipated… _____

My best choice of the day… _____

Date: _____

This is how my day went... _____

My sleep... _____

My stress level... _____

My mood... _____

My environment... _____

Breakfast... _____

Snack... _____

Lunch... _____

Dinner... _____

Snack... _____

Water Consumption... _____

This is how I plan to have a better day ... _____

My goal for the day... _____

Challenges anticipated... _____

My best choice of the day... _____

Date: _____

This is how my day went... _____

My sleep... _____

My stress level... _____

My mood... _____

My environment... _____

Breakfast... _____

Snack... _____

Lunch... _____

Dinner... _____

Snack... _____

Water Consumption... _____

This is how I plan to have a better day ... _____

My goal for the day... _____

Challenges anticipated... _____

My best choice of the day... _____

This week my…

Sleep: _____

Stress level: _____

Mood: _____

Environment: _____

Breakfast: _____

Lunch: _____

Dinner: _____

Snack: _____

Water consumption: _____

The week was _____

I need to improve on…

You rate yourself. Good/Bad, scale 1-10, yes/no, happy/sad, long short.
Did you eat the right foods, did you drink water? How was your stress level?

Things to Ponder

Reserve your bed for sleep and sex

Maintain a regular sleep wake schedule

Fall asleep by 10pm get up around 6am

Establish a regular relaxing bedtime routine
> *Soak in warm water*
> *Listen to soothing music*
> *Read a book*
> *Do what relaxes you*

Create a sleep friendly atmosphere that is quite, dark and cool and comfortable

Make your surroundings more sleep worthy

Invest in a comfortable mattress and pillow
> *It's worth the expense*

Eat 2-3 hours before bedtime

Exercise regularly

Date: _____

This is how my day went... _____

My sleep... _____

My stress level... _____

My mood... _____

My environment... _____

Breakfast... _____

Snack... _____

Lunch... _____

Dinner... _____

Snack... _____

Water Consumption... _____

This is how I plan to have a better day ... _____

My goal for the day... _____

Challenges anticipated... _____

My best choice of the day... _____

Date: _____

This is how my day went… _____

My sleep… _____

My stress level… _____

My mood… _____

My environment… _____

Breakfast… _____

Snack… _____

Lunch… _____

Dinner… _____

Snack… _____

Water Consumption… _____

This is how I plan to have a better day … _____

My goal for the day… _____

Challenges anticipated… _____

My best choice of the day… _____

Date: _____

This is how my day went... _____

My sleep... _____

My stress level... _____

My mood... _____

My environment... _____

Breakfast... _____

Snack... _____

Lunch... _____

Dinner... _____

Snack... _____

Water Consumption... _____

This is how I plan to have a better day ... _____

My goal for the day... _____

Challenges anticipated... _____

My best choice of the day... _____

Date: _____

This is how my day went... _____

My sleep... _____

My stress level... _____

My mood... _____

My environment... _____

Breakfast... _____

Snack... _____

Lunch... _____

Dinner... _____

Snack... _____

Water Consumption... _____

This is how I plan to have a better day ... _____

My goal for the day... _____

Challenges anticipated... _____

My best choice of the day... _____

Date: _____

This is how my day went... _____

My sleep... _____

My stress level... _____

My mood... _____

My environment... _____

Breakfast... _____

Snack... _____

Lunch... _____

Dinner... _____

Snack... _____

Water Consumption... _____

This is how I plan to have a better day ... _____

My goal for the day... _____

Challenges anticipated... _____

My best choice of the day... _____

Date: _____

This is how my day went... _____

My sleep... _____

My stress level... _____

My mood... _____

My environment... _____

Breakfast... _____

Snack... _____

Lunch... _____

Dinner... _____

Snack... _____

Water Consumption... _____

This is how I plan to have a better day ... _____

My goal for the day... _____

Challenges anticipated... _____

My best choice of the day... _____

Date: _____

This is how my day went... _____

My sleep... _____

My stress level... _____

My mood... _____

My environment... _____

Breakfast... _____

Snack... _____

Lunch... _____

Dinner... _____

Snack... _____

Water Consumption... _____

This is how I plan to have a better day ... _____

My goal for the day... _____

Challenges anticipated... _____

My best choice of the day... _____

Date: _____

This is how my day went… _____

My sleep… _____

My stress level… _____

My mood… _____

My environment… _____

Breakfast… _____

Snack… _____

Lunch… _____

Dinner… _____

Snack… _____

Water Consumption… _____

This is how I plan to have a better day … _____

My goal for the day… _____

Challenges anticipated… _____

My best choice of the day… _____

This week my...

    Sleep: _____

    Stress level: _____

    Mood: _____

    Environment: _____

    Breakfast: _____

    Lunch: _____

    Dinner: _____

    Snack: _____

    Water consumption: _____

        The week was _____

I need to improve on...

You rate yourself. Good/Bad, scale 1-10, yes/no, happy/sad, long short.
 Did you eat the right foods, did you drink water? How was your stress level?

Date: _____

This is how my day went... _____

My sleep... _____

My stress level... _____

My mood... _____

My environment... _____

Breakfast... _____

Snack... _____

Lunch... _____

Dinner... _____

Snack... _____

Water Consumption... _____

This is how I plan to have a better day ... _____

My goal for the day... _____

Challenges anticipated... _____

My best choice of the day... _____

Date: _____

This is how my day went... _____

My sleep... _____

My stress level... _____

My mood... _____

My environment... _____

Breakfast... _____

Snack... _____

Lunch... _____

Dinner... _____

Snack... _____

Water Consumption... _____

This is how I plan to have a better day ... _____

My goal for the day... _____

Challenges anticipated... _____

My best choice of the day... _____

Date: _____

This is how my day went… _____

My sleep… _____

My stress level… _____

My mood… _____

My environment… _____

Breakfast… _____

Snack… _____

Lunch… _____

Dinner… _____

Snack… _____

Water Consumption… _____

This is how I plan to have a better day … _____

My goal for the day… _____

Challenges anticipated… _____

My best choice of the day… _____

Date: _____

This is how my day went… _____

My sleep… _____

My stress level… _____

My mood… _____

My environment… _____

Breakfast… _____

Snack… _____

Lunch… _____

Dinner… _____

Snack… _____

Water Consumption… _____

This is how I plan to have a better day … _____

My goal for the day… _____

Challenges anticipated… _____

My best choice of the day… _____

Date: _____

This is how my day went... _____

My sleep... _____

My stress level... _____

My mood... _____

My environment... _____

Breakfast... _____

Snack... _____

Lunch... _____

Dinner... _____

Snack... _____

Water Consumption... _____

This is how I plan to have a better day ... _____

My goal for the day... _____

Challenges anticipated... _____

My best choice of the day... _____

Date: _____

This is how my day went... _____

My sleep... _____

My stress level... _____

My mood... _____

My environment... _____

Breakfast... _____

Snack... _____

Lunch... _____

Dinner... _____

Snack... _____

Water Consumption... _____

This is how I plan to have a better day ... _____

My goal for the day... _____

Challenges anticipated... _____

My best choice of the day... _____

Date: _____

This is how my day went... _____

My sleep... _____

My stress level... _____

My mood... _____

My environment... _____

Breakfast... _____

Snack... _____

Lunch... _____

Dinner... _____

Snack... _____

Water Consumption... _____

This is how I plan to have a better day ... _____

My goal for the day... _____

Challenges anticipated... _____

My best choice of the day... _____

This week my...

Sleep: _____

Stress level: _____

Mood: _____

Environment: _____

Breakfast: _____

Lunch: _____

Dinner: _____

Snack: _____

Water consumption: _____

The week was _____

I need to improve on...

You rate yourself. Good/Bad, scale 1-10, yes/no, happy/sad, long short.
Did you eat the right foods, did you drink water? How was your stress level?

Date: _____

This is how my day went... _____

My sleep... _____

My stress level... _____

My mood... _____

My environment... _____

Breakfast... _____

Snack... _____

Lunch... _____

Dinner... _____

Snack... _____

Water Consumption... _____

This is how I plan to have a better day ... _____

My goal for the day... _____

Challenges anticipated... _____

My best choice of the day... _____

Date: _____

This is how my day went... _____

My sleep... _____

My stress level... _____

My mood... _____

My environment... _____

Breakfast... _____

Snack... _____

Lunch... _____

Dinner... _____

Snack... _____

Water Consumption... _____

This is how I plan to have a better day ... _____

My goal for the day... _____

Challenges anticipated... _____

My best choice of the day... _____

Date: _____

This is how my day went... _____

My sleep... _____

My stress level... _____

My mood... _____

My environment... _____

Breakfast... _____

Snack... _____

Lunch... _____

Dinner... _____

Snack... _____

Water Consumption... _____

This is how I plan to have a better day ... _____

My goal for the day... _____

Challenges anticipated... _____

My best choice of the day... _____

Date: _____

This is how my day went... _____

My sleep... _____

My stress level... _____

My mood... _____

My environment... _____

Breakfast... _____

Snack... _____

Lunch... _____

Dinner... _____

Snack... _____

Water Consumption... _____

This is how I plan to have a better day ... _____

My goal for the day... _____

Challenges anticipated... _____

My best choice of the day... _____

Date: _____

This is how my day went... _____

My sleep... _____

My stress level... _____

My mood... _____

My environment... _____

Breakfast... _____

Snack... _____

Lunch... _____

Dinner... _____

Snack... _____

Water Consumption... _____

This is how I plan to have a better day ... _____

My goal for the day... _____

Challenges anticipated... _____

My best choice of the day... _____

This week my…

Sleep: _____

Stress level: _____

Mood: _____

Environment: _____

Breakfast: _____

Lunch: _____

Dinner: _____

Snack: _____

Water consumption: _____

The week was _____

I need to improve on…

You rate yourself. Good/Bad, scale 1-10, yes/no, happy/sad, long short.
Did you eat the right foods, did you drink water? How was your stress level?

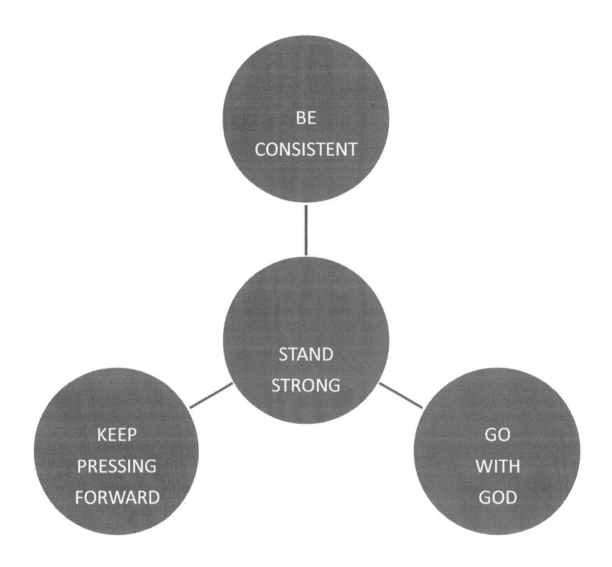

Date: _____

This is how my day went... _____

My sleep... _____

My stress level... _____

My mood... _____

My environment... _____

Breakfast... _____

Snack... _____

Lunch... _____

Dinner... _____

Snack... _____

Water Consumption... _____

This is what I plan to have a better day ... _____

My goal for the day... _____

Challenges anticipated... _____

My best choice for the day... _____

Date: _____

This is how my day went... _____

My sleep... _____

My stress level... _____

My mood... _____

My environment... _____

Breakfast... _____

Snack... _____

Lunch... _____

Dinner... _____

Snack... _____

Water Consumption... _____

This is how I plan to have a better day ... _____

My goal for the day... _____

Challenges anticipated... _____

My best choice of the day... _____

Date: _____

This is how my day went... _____

My sleep... _____

My stress level... _____

My mood... _____

My environment... _____

Breakfast... _____

Snack... _____

Lunch... _____

Dinner... _____

Snack... _____

Water Consumption... _____

This is how I plan to have a better day ... _____

My goal for the day... _____

Challenges anticipated... _____

My best choice of the day... _____

Date: _____

This is how my day went... _____

My sleep... _____

My stress level... _____

My mood... _____

My environment... _____

Breakfast... _____

Snack... _____

Lunch... _____

Dinner... _____

Snack... _____

Water Consumption... _____

This is how I plan to have a better day ... _____

My goal for the day... _____

Challenges anticipated... _____

My best choice of the day... _____

Date: _____

This is how my day went... _____

My sleep... _____

My stress level... _____

My mood... _____

My environment... _____

Breakfast... _____

Snack... _____

Lunch... _____

Dinner... _____

Snack... _____

Water Consumption... _____

This is how I plan to have a better day ... _____

My goal for the day... _____

Challenges anticipated... _____

My best choice of the day... _____

This week my…

Sleep: _____

Stress level: _____

Mood: _____

Environment: _____

Breakfast: _____

Lunch: _____

Dinner: _____

Snack: _____

Water consumption: _____

The week was _____

I need to improve on…

You rate yourself. Good/Bad, scale 1-10, yes/no, happy/sad, long short.
 Did you eat the right foods, did you drink water? How was your stress level?

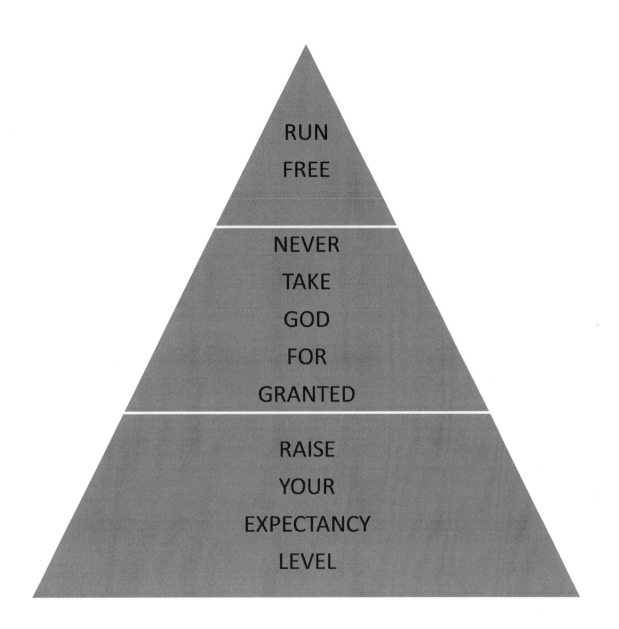

RUN

FREE

NEVER

TAKE

GOD

FOR

GRANTED

RAISE

YOUR

EXPECTANCY

LEVEL

Date: _____

This is how my day went… _____

My sleep… _____

My stress level… _____

My mood… _____

My environment… _____

Breakfast… _____

Snack… _____

Lunch… _____

Dinner… _____

Snack… _____

Water Consumption… _____

This is how I plan to have a better day … _____

My goal for the day… _____

Challenges anticipated… _____

My best choice of the day… _____

Date: _____

This is how my day went... _____

My sleep... _____

My stress level... _____

My mood... _____

My environment... _____

Breakfast... _____

Snack... _____

Lunch... _____

Dinner... _____

Snack... _____

Water Consumption... _____

This is how I plan to have a better day ... _____

My goal for the day... _____

Challenges anticipated... _____

My best choice of the day... _____

Date: _____

This is how my day went... _____

My sleep... _____

My stress level... _____

My mood... _____

My environment... _____

Breakfast... _____

Snack... _____

Lunch... _____

Dinner... _____

Snack... _____

Water Consumption... _____

This is how I plan to have a better day ... _____

My goal for the day... _____

Challenges anticipated... _____

My best choice of the day... _____

Date: _____

This is how my day went... _____

My sleep... _____

My stress level... _____

My mood... _____

My environment... _____

Breakfast... _____

Snack... _____

Lunch... _____

Dinner... _____

Snack... _____

Water Consumption... _____

This is how I plan to have a better day ... _____

My goal for the day... _____

Challenges anticipated... _____

My best choice of the day... _____

Date: _____

This is how my day went... _____

My sleep... _____

My stress level... _____

My mood... _____

My environment... _____

Breakfast... _____

Snack... _____

Lunch... _____

Dinner... _____

Snack... _____

Water Consumption... _____

This is how I plan to have a better day ... _____

My goal for the day... _____

Challenges anticipated... _____

My best choice of the day... _____

Date: _____

This is how my day went... _____

My sleep... _____

My stress level... _____

My mood... _____

My environment... _____

Breakfast... _____

Snack... _____

Lunch... _____

Dinner... _____

Snack... _____

Water Consumption... _____

This is how I plan to have a better day ... _____

My goal for the day... _____

Challenges anticipated... _____

My best choice of the day... _____

Date: _____

This is how my day went... _____

My sleep... _____

My stress level... _____

My mood... _____

My environment... _____

Breakfast... _____

Snack... _____

Lunch... _____

Dinner... _____

Snack... _____

Water Consumption... _____

This is how I plan to have a better day ... _____

My goal for the day... _____

Challenges anticipated... _____

My best choice of the day... _____

This week my…

    Sleep: _____

    Stress level: _____

    Mood: _____

    Environment: _____

    Breakfast: _____

    Lunch: _____

    Dinner: _____

    Snack: _____

    Water consumption: _____

        The week was _____

I need to improve on…

You rate yourself. Good/Bad, scale 1-10, yes/no, happy/sad, long short.
Did you eat the right foods, did you drink water? How was your stress level?

Date: _____

This is how my day went... _____

My sleep... _____

My stress level... _____

My mood... _____

My environment... _____

Breakfast... _____

Snack... _____

Lunch... _____

Dinner... _____

Snack... _____

Water Consumption... _____

This is how I plan to have a better day ... _____

My goal for the day... _____

Challenges anticipated... _____

My best choice of the day... _____

Date: _____

This is how my day went... _____

My sleep... _____

My stress level... _____

My mood... _____

My environment... _____

Breakfast... _____

Snack... _____

Lunch... _____

Dinner... _____

Snack... _____

Water Consumption... _____

This is how I plan to have a better day ... _____

My goal for the day... _____

Challenges anticipated... _____

My best choice of the day... _____

Date: _____

This is how my day went... _____

My sleep... _____

My stress level... _____

My mood... _____

My environment... _____

Breakfast... _____

Snack... _____

Lunch... _____

Dinner... _____

Snack... _____

Water Consumption... _____

This is how I plan to have a better day ... _____

My goal for the day... _____

Challenges anticipated... _____

My best choice of the day... _____

Date: _____

This is how my day went... _____

My sleep... _____

My stress level... _____

My mood... _____

My environment... _____

Breakfast... _____

Snack... _____

Lunch... _____

Dinner... _____

Snack... _____

Water Consumption... _____

This is how I plan to have a better day ... _____

My goal for the day... _____

Challenges anticipated... _____

My best choice of the day... _____

This week my…

Sleep: _____

Stress level: _____

Mood: _____

Environment: _____

Breakfast: _____

Lunch: _____

Dinner: _____

Snack: _____

Water consumption: _____

The week was _____

I need to improve on…

You rate yourself. Good/Bad, scale 1-10, yes/no, happy/sad, long short.
Did you eat the right foods, did you drink water? How was your stress level?

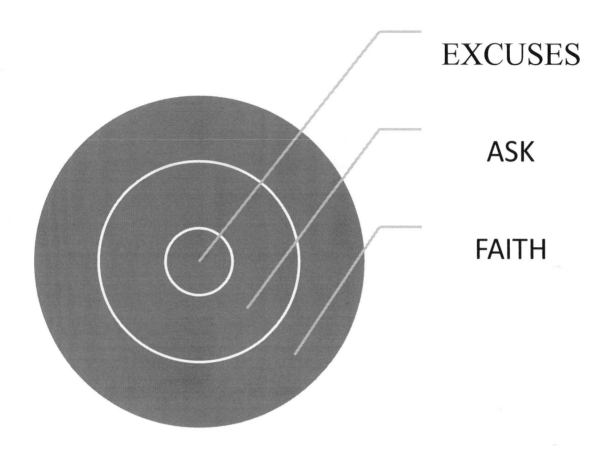

EXCUSES

ASK

FAITH

EXCUSES: should be minimal
ASK: as many questions you can think of
FAITH: have abundant faith

WHERE ARE YOU IN YOUR LIFE

WHAT DO YOU WANT TO ACCOMPLISH

LIVE LIFE TO THE FULLEST

SMILE
LAUGH
GIVE A HUG
WAVE AT THE KIDS ON THE SCHOOL BUS
TREAT YOURSELF
BE HUMBLE

Date: _____

This is how my day went... _____

My sleep... _____

My stress level... _____

My mood... _____

My environment... _____

Breakfast... _____

Snack... _____

Lunch... _____

Dinner... _____

Snack... _____

Water Consumption... _____

This is how I plan to have a better day ... _____

My goal for the day... _____

Challenges anticipated... _____

My best choice of the day... _____

Date: _____

This is how my day went... _____

My sleep... _____

My stress level... _____

My mood... _____

My environment... _____

Breakfast... _____

Snack... _____

Lunch... _____

Dinner... _____

Snack... _____

Water Consumption... _____

This is how I plan to have a better day ... _____

My goal for the day... _____

Challenges anticipated... _____

My best choice of the day... _____

Date: _____

This is how my day went... _____

My sleep... _____

My stress level... _____

My mood... _____

My environment... _____

Breakfast... _____

Snack... _____

Lunch... _____

Dinner... _____

Snack... _____

Water Consumption... _____

This is how I plan to have a better day ... _____

My goal for the day... _____

Challenges anticipated... _____

My best choice of the day... _____

Date: _____

This is how my day went... _____

My sleep... _____

My stress level... _____

My mood... _____

My environment... _____

Breakfast... _____

Snack... _____

Lunch... _____

Dinner... _____

Snack... _____

Water Consumption... _____

This is how I plan to have a better day ... _____

My goal for the day... _____

Challenges anticipated... _____

My best choice of the day... _____

Date: _____

This is how my day went... _____

My sleep... _____

My stress level... _____

My mood... _____

My environment... _____

Breakfast... _____

Snack... _____

Lunch... _____

Dinner... _____

Snack... _____

Water Consumption... _____

This is how I plan to have a better day ... _____

My goal for the day... _____

Challenges anticipated... _____

My best choice of the day... _____

Date: _____

This is how my day went... _____

My sleep... _____

My stress level... _____

My mood... _____

My environment... _____

Breakfast... _____

Snack... _____

Lunch... _____

Dinner... _____

Snack... _____

Water Consumption... _____

This is how I plan to have a better day ... _____

My goal for the day... _____

Challenges anticipated... _____

My best choice of the day... _____

This week my…

Sleep: _____

Stress level: _____

Mood: _____

Environment: _____

Breakfast: _____

Lunch: _____

Dinner: _____

Snack: _____

Water consumption: _____

The week was _____

I need to improve on…

You rate yourself. Good/Bad, scale 1-10, yes/no, happy/sad, long short.
Did you eat the right foods, did you drink water? How was your stress level?

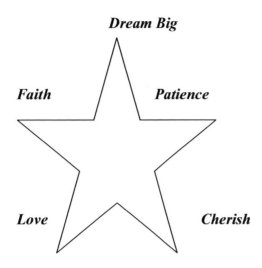

Be honest with yourself when you answer these questions

- Do you eat at least 5 servings of vegetables and fruits every day?
- Do you eat at least 3 servings of whole grain bread, rice, pasta, and cereal every day?
- Do you drink reduced fat or fat free milk and yogurt?
- Do you eat high calorie bake goods (doughnuts, cookies, pies, sweet rolls)
- Do you eat processed and red meat like bacon, hot dogs, sausage, steak ground beef, pork or lamb?
- Do you try to maintain a healthy weight?
- Do you take the stairs instead of waiting for the elevator?
- Do you spend of most of your free time being active, instead of watching television or sitting at the computer?
- Do you get at least 30 minutes of moderate to vigorous physical activity on 5 or more days a week

Now look at your answers and see where you can improve

- Do you need to eat more vegetables and fruits
- Do you need to add whole grains to your diet
- Do you need to monitor the fat and meat in your diet
- Do you need to increase your physical activity

Your on your way to a healthy you

What's a portion size (control?)

 = 1 cup of vegetables or fruit

 = medium apple or orange

 = medium potato

 = palm of hand portion of meat, chicken, fish

 = volume of pasta, oatmeal

Date: _____

This is how my day went... _____

My sleep... _____

My stress level... _____

My mood... _____

My environment... _____

Breakfast... _____

Snack... _____

Lunch... _____

Dinner... _____

Snack... _____

Water Consumption... _____

This is how I plan to have a better day ... _____

My goal for the day... _____

Challenges anticipated... _____

My best choice of the day... _____

Date: _____

This is how my day went… _____

My sleep… _____

My stress level… _____

My mood… _____

My environment… _____

Breakfast… _____

Snack… _____

Lunch… _____

Dinner… _____

Snack… _____

Water Consumption… _____

This is how I plan to have a better day … _____

My goal for the day… _____

Challenges anticipated… _____

My best choice of the day… _____

Date: _____

This is how my day went... _____

My sleep... _____

My stress level... _____

My mood... _____

My environment... _____

Breakfast... _____

Snack... _____

Lunch... _____

Dinner... _____

Snack... _____

Water Consumption... _____

This is how I plan to have a better day ... _____

My goal for the day... _____

Challenges anticipated... _____

My best choice of the day... _____

Date: _____

This is how my day went... _____

My sleep... _____

My stress level... _____

My mood... _____

My environment... _____

Breakfast... _____

Snack... _____

Lunch... _____

Dinner... _____

Snack... _____

Water Consumption... _____

This is how I plan to have a better day ... _____

My goal for the day... _____

Challenges anticipated... _____

My best choice of the day... _____

Date: _____

This is how my day went... _____

My sleep... _____

My stress level... _____

My mood... _____

My environment... _____

Breakfast... _____

Snack... _____

Lunch... _____

Dinner... _____

Snack... _____

Water Consumption... _____

This is how I plan to have a better day ... _____

My goal for the day... _____

Challenges anticipated... _____

My best choice of the day... _____

Date: _____

This is how my day went... _____

My sleep... _____

My stress level... _____

My mood... _____

My environment... _____

Breakfast... _____

Snack... _____

Lunch... _____

Dinner... _____

Snack... _____

Water Consumption... _____

This is how I plan to have a better day ... _____

My goal for the day... _____

Challenges anticipated... _____

My best choice of the day... _____

Date: _____

This is how my day went... _____

My sleep... _____

My stress level... _____

My mood... _____

My environment... _____

Breakfast... _____

Snack... _____

Lunch... _____

Dinner... _____

Snack... _____

Water Consumption... _____

This is how I plan to have a better day ... _____

My goal for the day... _____

Challenges anticipated... _____

My best choice of the day... _____

This week my...

Sleep: _____

Stress level: _____

Mood: _____

Environment: _____

Breakfast: _____

Lunch: _____

Dinner: _____

Snack: _____

Water consumption: _____

The week was _____

I need to improve on...

You rate yourself. Good/Bad, scale 1-10, yes/no, happy/sad, long short.
 Did you eat the right foods, did you drink water? How was your stress level?

BRAIN TEASERS

STIMULATE YOUR BRAIN

If you are right handed use your left hand
If your are left handed use your right hand
(Get the picture)

TAKE YOGA
TRY A DIFFERENT FOOD
TRY A NEW RESTAURANT
LEARN TO READ A MAP
TAKE A TRIP
SMILE
LAUGH
HUG
GIVE THANKS
SAY SORRY (AND MEAN IT)
SAY SOMETHING POSITIVE
HOST A DINNER
HOST A LUNCH
HOST A BREAKFAST

MOST OF ALL LOVE YOURSELF

THE BEGINING

May your life be inspired by each day you journal
May God's blessing uplift you
May your Angel guide you through life's changes

Happy Journaling

Brenda

Place thoughts and prayers that come to you while your journaling here:

_____

_____

_____

_____

_____

_____

_____

_____

_____

_____

_____

_____

_____

_____

_____

_____

Made in the USA
Charleston, SC
20 January 2011